Reeves Turtle as Pets

The Ultimate Reeves Turtle Manual

Reeves Turtle General Info, Purchasing, Care, Cost, Keeping, Health, Supplies, Food, Breeding and More Included!

By: Lolly Brown

Copyrights and Trademarks

All rights reserved. No part of this book may be reproduced or transformed in any form or by any means, graphic, electronic, or mechanical, including photocopying, recording, taping, or by any information storage retrieval system, without the written permission of the author.

This publication is Copyright ©2019 NRB Publishing, an imprint. Nevada. All products, graphics, publications, software and services mentioned and recommended in this publication are protected by trademarks. In such instance, all trademarks & copyright belong to the respective owners. For information consult www.NRBpublishing.com

Disclaimer and Legal Notice

This product is not legal, medical, or accounting advice and should not be interpreted in that manner. You need to do your own due-diligence to determine if the content of this product is right for you. While every attempt has been made to verify the information shared in this publication, neither the author, neither publisher, nor the affiliates assume any responsibility for errors, omissions or contrary interpretation of the subject matter herein. Any perceived slights to any specific person(s) or organization(s) are purely unintentional.

We have no control over the nature, content and availability of the web sites listed in this book. The inclusion of any web site links does not necessarily imply a recommendation or endorse the views expressed within them. We take no responsibility for, and will not be liable for, the websites being temporarily unavailable or being removed from the internet.

The accuracy and completeness of information provided herein and opinions stated herein are not guaranteed or warranted to produce any particular results, and the advice and strategies, contained herein may not be suitable for every individual. Neither the author nor the publisher shall be liable for any loss incurred as a consequence of the use and application, directly or indirectly, of any information presented in this work. This publication is designed to provide information in regard to the subject matter covered.

Neither the author nor the publisher assume any responsibility for any errors or omissions, nor do they represent or warrant that the ideas, information, actions, plans, suggestions contained in this book is in all cases accurate. It is the reader's responsibility to find advice before putting anything written in this book into practice. The information in this book is not intended to serve as legal, medical, or accounting advice.

Foreword

A pet is a lifetime companion that would surely spice up your life. It would light up your life by adding a companion or even adding it as a family member. Each member of the family will surely enjoy your pet.

A key into finding the best pet possible way is learning something about it. You must know the ins and the outs of the pet before you even bring it at home. Other than that, you and your family members should agree on all things about this pet as well as having enough space to raise your pet.

One of the best pets you can ever own is a turtle. A turtle is considered to be a low maintenance pet. Unlike other commercially available pet, you just need to set-up a liveable habitat, feed it every day, and you are off to go. You do not really need to spend time with it for it not to get lonely and bored. This characteristic is what makes a turtle a top choice for some pet owners.

Reeves turtle is pretty uncommon to people. They are unsure of its traits, habitat, and overall health issues. However, this kind of turtle is one of the best ones that you can own. This book will help you explore all information available for this type of turtle. We will persuade you that getting a Reeves Turtle is one of the best life choices that you can have.

Table of Contents

Chapter One: Thinking of Keeping a Reeves Turtle? 9

Chapter Two: Choosing Reeves Turtles as Pets 13

    What Makes It a Great Pet 14

    The Value of Money 20

    How Much is Truly Enough? 20

    Housing Needs 23

    Lighting and Temperature 25

    Water Supply 26

    Food Requirements 28

Chapter Three: A Suitable Habitat for your Reeves Turtle .. 31

    Housing Needs 33

    What You Need to Set Up a Turtle Habitat 34

        Terrarium Starter Kits 37

    Choosing a Tank Substrate 46

    Other Essential Things That You Will Need 48

    Quality of Water 49

        How to Measure Quality of Water 50

        Do I Need To Mind Chlorine in Water? 51

        Salmonella Warning 52

    The Correct Tank Size: How Big Should I Get? 52

The Filtration System 53

    Partial Water Changes 53

Cleaning your Turtle Aquarium 56

Tank Cleaning 101 57

The Basics of Tank Cleaning 57

    Cleaning the Tank 60

Chapter Four: Meal Plan to Your Reeves Turtle 65

Food for My Reeves Turtle 66

    Some Food Suggestions 67

Chapter Five: Life Cycle of Your Reeves Turtle 71

Life Cycle 72

    The First Step of Their Lives: Eggs 72

    The Second Step: Becoming a Hatchling 72

    The Highlight: Turtle as Adults 73

Breeding Time 73

Chapter Six: Keeping Your Reeves Turtle Healthy 79

Inspect the Turtle Aquarium 80

Handling and Grooming 86

Chapter Seven: Medical Problems of Reeves Turtles 93

Turtle Vitamin A Deficiency 94

Aural or Ear Abscesses in Turtles 95

Respiratory Tract Disease in Turtles 95

Turtle Trauma 96

Turtle Impaction 98

Turtle Egg - Binding 99

Turtle Shell Lesions 99

Other Problems That Your Pet Might Face 100

Prevention is the Key to All 105

Conclusion 107

Keep in Mind! 108

Glossary of Amphibian Terms 111

Photo Credits 117

References 118

Chapter One: Thinking of Keeping a Reeves Turtle?

The Reeves Turtle is considered to be one of the easiest turtle to take care of. It is just a breeze to take care of that you would not really remember having it as a pet.

Unlike typical household pets, your Reeves Turtle need specific things to have a happy life. First of all, you need to give it a house that would mimic its natural environment. Tasking as it sound, making a terrarium would be one of the greatest symbol of love that you can give to your pet.

Chapter One: Thinking of Keeping a Reeves Turtle?

In addition to that, you should be the one to know all the health restrictions for your pet. Know what are the good things and the bad things for your pet. Do not give foods that are considered unhealthy for them. Remember, you are keeping them in a cage; they do not have a lot of food choices inside the terrarium.

Other than that, you should also know the terrarium set-up. Do not go all fancy just like you see things in several sites. Make the terrarium work for both you and your pet. You do not want a terrarium that is fancy but is very difficult to maintain, right?

Also note that having a turtle would not only having it during the happy times, know that you should also be present during the bad days in its life. It can't really complain about its problem, it can't voice out how if feels. You must be sensitive enough to know what is wrong for your turtle. Do not try home remedies because you might only make things work. Always have this handy book in hand to know what you need to do when a problem arises.

There might be a lot of things that you need to do, however, having a pet is surely a blast in the long run. You

Chapter One: Thinking of Keeping a Reeves Turtle?

would not be alone in your house anymore! Let us begin our wonderful journey as Reeves turtle pet owners!

Chapter One: Thinking of Keeping a Reeves Turtle?

Chapter Two: Choosing Reeves Turtles as Pets

The first chapter has dwelt with the basics of the Reeves Turtle; we have given you its basic characteristics and its short but rich background. The first chapter has also given you quick facts that you need to remember every time you need to take care of your pet.

In this chapter, we will be talking about the behavioural traits, budgets, and other necessary things about the Reeves Turtle. These things might entice you to have your own turtle in the near future.

Chapter Two: Choosing Reeves Turtles as Pets

There are still a lot of things that you need to know about the Reeves Turtle. You might think that this turtle is just easy to take care of, but you need to prepare not only yourself but also your home if you want to welcome a Reeves Turtle in your homes.

What Makes It a Great Pet

A pet is an addition for a single or even a family household. It would really spark up your world and give your life a little more thrill. Just like in any decision that you will make, you need to think things through before bringing it home. Remember, adding a pet is just like welcoming a new baby into the house. Make sure you are financially and mentally ready.

After you have chosen your desired pet, you need to put all effort into taking care of your pet. You need to be ready with your budget as well as time to give the best time for your pet.

Chapter Two: Choosing Reeves Turtles as Pets

A Reeves Turtle is one of the best choices for beginner turtle owners. However, some people are still scared in taking care of turtles. You need to provide the same environment your turtle has in its wildlife state. It might be difficult at first, but you would surely learn from it.

Temperament and Behavioral Characteristics

- ✓ They are not social animals.
- ✓ These turtles could cohabitate with the same specie or even other specie just with the same habitat needs.
- ✓ Both male and female could be very territorial or dominant in terms of aggression, but this could not give serious injury as long as you provide enough hiding areas and space.
- ✓ You need to provide a big house so your turtles could not offend other turtles especially if you can see aggression from your pets.
- ✓ Reeves Turtle is not a domesticated animal; they do not love human contact and affection, and they should not be handled except it is extremely necessary.
- ✓ You should only handle these turtles to inspect their

Chapter Two: Choosing Reeves Turtles as Pets

injuries or health; aside from that, they should only be handled for relocation of your pets.

✓ Handling your Reeves Turtle could be very stressful for your pet. It could scratch or even bite you; thoroughly wash your hand before and after handling so you will not get any disease from your pet.

These are just some of the basic behavioral characteristics of your Reeves Turtle. There are other traits that we have not tackled; however, you could know these characteristics and traits as you raise your Reeves Turtle on your own.

Why Own A Turtle?

Every one of us has dreamed of owning a turtle at any part of our lives. You could have woken up one day and realized that you want to have a turtle in your life.

Here are some reasons why you might want to own a turtle now:

1. Reeves Turtles are Adorable

Turtles are considered to be little cute creatures.

Chapter Two: Choosing Reeves Turtles as Pets

However, they still have a lot of personality. This specific kind of turtle does not like to be taken out of their habitat or even played with. You can still look at them in the eyes and see if they do not like you. You could still see them have fun and grow up into an adult turtle.

2. They are somehow cheap.

Reeves Turtles are cheaper compared to your other household pet. You can easily find them in most pet stores and once set - up, they are relatively easy to take care of.

3. Reeves Turtles are low maintenance pets.

Once you have given them the correct habitat, as well as food and enough space, they are relatively easy to maintain. You can even go on a number of days without looking them up.

4. They are, generally, harmless.

Your Reeves Turtle is generally harmless. They would not really scratch or even bite you for no reason at all. This goes great for families with small children. You can find

Chapter Two: Choosing Reeves Turtles as Pets

harmless turtles in pet stores.

5. They could teach you responsibility.

When you own a pet, it could teach you to become responsible. It could teach you to take care something aside from yourself. They are typically easier than your dog, but it is just as important.

6. They are always there to listen to you.

You could always count on your pet to listen to your problems. They always have a listening ear ready for anything that you would share with it.

These are just some of the reasons why you should own a Reeves Turtle now. However, there are certain personal testaments that you could still search over the net.

If there are positive reasons to own pet, there are still reasons why you should not own your Reeves Turtle. Be open to these things because you might also experience these too.

Chapter Two: Choosing Reeves Turtles as Pets

The have a tendency to escape their aquariums.

When your pet starts to know how to dig around their aquarium, they might be very difficult to contain. They might escape their aquariums easily.

Aside from that, they won't come out of their shells for a period of time. So you need to be patient with their attitude.

It is very difficult to clean and maintain them.

Because you are giving them their own habitat, it might be difficult for you to always clean and arrange all the things around the terrarium. You need to find the balance between the things and make sure you remember where the specific things are.

You have now probably made up your mind that you want to own a Reeves Turtle, especially after going through the list we have given you. Aside from these considerations, you need to know other costs to own your pet before you even purchase it.

The Value of Money

Having a pet in your life requires a lot of thing. You need to find the best place to buy your Reeves Turtle, as well as the place to buy tank or aquarium, water dishes and food bowls, and other daily supplies for your pet. Remember, having a pet is just like raising your own kid in your life.

This portion will help you see how much you need you need in order to have a good budget for your Reeves Turtle.

How Much is Truly Enough?

A new pet in your midst is never easy. You need to prepare everything before you bring in your companion in your life. A new pet is like having a child, you need to provide it with shelter, water, food, and other necessities deemed necessary. For this reason, you need to allot a specific budget for this task.

Chapter Two: Choosing Reeves Turtles as Pets

Budgeting your money for your new companion might be difficult at first, but you will soon learn it if you plan it well in the early stages.

The overall cost of owning your Reeves Turtle would heavily depend on the number and quality of the needs that you will be buying. If you will be buying great quality products, it might be more expensive. However, this product may last you for a long time. If you will buy a cheap product, that you need to buy over and over again - it is not worth it.

This portion will give you a detailed analysis for the budget of your pet.

Reeve's Turtle Price

The price of your Reeves Turtle would greatly differ when it comes to the gender and age of your pet. However, you should still find the best Reeves Turtle possible before you go out and buy your pet.

Typically, your Reeves Turtle would be around $70 to $500. The price depends on the gender and the age of your

Chapter Two: Choosing Reeves Turtles as Pets

pet. A great factor would also be the place where you would buy it.

A hatchling might be cheaper than an old turtle, but a hatchling is more difficult to take care of. In whatever choice you might want to be prepared to shell out the money.

Look for a reputable breeder in your area. Ask essential questions before you set your mind on buying your pet.

Other Essentials

Buying the Reeves Turtle is only the first step in the game. You should be financially ready with all the essentials that you need to have before you bring you pet at home.

There are allotted things that you need to have in order to keep your pet healthy and alive. Some of these things are only one time purchases such as tanks, heating pads, filters. While some things are recurrent expenses, such as food and supplements. But these things are needed for your pet to have a complete nutrition and a happy life.

Chapter Two: Choosing Reeves Turtles as Pets

Lucky for you, most of these things are easily available in your area. Find out the best brand and kind and go out and buy these essential things today.

Housing Needs

Your Reeves Turtles are not really great swimmers, especially if you compare it to other turtles such as Sliders, Map Turtles, and etc. These turtles could still swim in deep water, provided that you give them an access to the land.

When creating a terrarium for your turtle, you should put driftwood or any similar structure that could be used as your as resting sites in the water region.

Your hatchlings should always be kept in low water; they should be able to breathe without the hassle of swimming. You can put plastic plants or even live plants that are floating.

When your turtle is already old, it will need an aquarium with 20-30 gallons. Remember, the bigger the aquarium, the better. You can put a big portion for the water and land area in the said aquarium.

Chapter Two: Choosing Reeves Turtles as Pets

Koi ponds or even wading pools can be refurbished into a great habitat for your Reeves Turtle. It is best to have outdoor housing; you just need to make sure that there are no predators or raccoons around.

Wild Reeves Turtle typically spend their time on land; captive turtles should be kept in a half-and-half environment, except when you can't provide access to both land and water area.

In the terrarium, it should have a dry basking surface. Turtle ramps and docs that are commercially available may work for smaller turtles; however, adults may sink if the basking area is not properly adhered to the glass. You can even put cork bark that is wedged between the sides of the aquarium.

You can keep your Reeves Turtle in a bare-bottomed aquarium. Gravels may trap waste material, it would surely complicate the cleaning procedure or your pet may even swallow it.

Chapter Two: Choosing Reeves Turtles as Pets

Lighting and Temperature

You need to provide your Reeves Turtle with UVB light source. You can give natural sun light, however, it must be direct as plastic and glass may filter the needed UVB rays.

You can also use a florescent bulb, but you need to make sure that you put a basking area within six to 12 inches of it. Vapor bulbs with mercury are a great source of UVB lights, which they could even emit at a greater distance. Mercury Vapor Bulbs and Halogen Bulbs will also provide UVA light which is beneficial to your pets. You should get water resistant bulbs if you plan to have both water and land section in your aquarium.

You should maintain a water temperature of 75 to 82 F throughout the aquarium. You should put an incandescent light bulb with a temperature of 90 F on the basking site of the terrarium.

During day light, your turtle might move periodically to the basking area. They will do this to warm up, dry themselves, rest, and even absorb UVB light.

Chapter Two: Choosing Reeves Turtles as Pets

Your turtle's basking spot should be around 80 F, aside from this, it should have enough UV. Your turtle needs an additional UVB light which some lights could not produce.

Your Reeves Turtle requires UVB light to synthesize vitamin D. Without this kind of vitamin (especially vitamin D3), your turtle could not metabolize calcium properly and might cause problems with bone growth.

You can use a UV tube and even a spot light in the basking area of the aquarium. Make sure you use either a 100w or a 60w bulb but still could maintain the specific temperature.

You can use a 12% intense UV tube to provide a lot of UV light. You could also use one mercury vapor bulb to provide both UV and heat. You should put this bulb around 30 cm or even closer, you need a ceramic or porcelain lamp holder for this kind of light.

Water Supply

Your Reeves Turtle likes to spend time on water, for this reason, you should keep the water clean and warm --

Chapter Two: Choosing Reeves Turtles as Pets

this should be your number one priority.

Your pet could be very messy because of their high protein diet; you need to purchase a strong filter to clean the water efficiently. If you have bought an amazing water filter, you would be at peace and you would just check the water once in a while and even clean the entire terrarium for every three months or even longer.

You should always treat water before you even introduce it to your turtles, this act would remove the chlorine. If you fail to treat water, some trace elements in your tap water could possible disturb your turtle's biological pads inside your filter and it might even affect your pet.

You should have a constant water temperature of 25 C. This temperature should be maintained during the night and even the day. You can use a water heater in order to keep the water warm. Remember, every one litter of water could be warmed by a 1W bulb. If you have a larger enclosure, those over 3ft, you should buy two half strength water heaters. Place these water heaters at each end of the enclosure to ensure that there is even temperature inside the terrarium.

Food Requirements

Your Reeves Turtle could eat many types of food; this could range from meat products, aquatic food, and even live food. You could also feed dried food if there is no live or fresh food available near you. You can create dried food with meat protein or shrimp, but not vegetation.

You can easily give brown crickets to your Reeves Turtle. However, you could also give dubia cockroaches, black crickets, or hoppers (locusts). You could also give salmon, shrimp, chicks, and mice as the meat portion of your Reeves Turtle diet.

These are just some basic necessities that you need to prepare once you make up your mind that you really want to own a Reeves Turtle.

Remember, you need to have these things ready before you even bring home your pet so you will not have any other issues.

Chapter Two: Choosing Reeves Turtles as Pets

You may ask your vet or even some breeders on their ideas and suggestions on the brands and supplies that they have used for their terrarium.

Chapter Two: Choosing Reeves Turtles as Pets

Chapter Three: A Suitable Habitat for your Reeves Turtle

You have now decided that you want to own a Reeves Turtle. We have already discussed all the background information about the pet, aside from that; we have given you all the necessities to set up before bringing in your pet.

You need to also ask your vet and even other breeders on other essentials for your pet Reeves Turtle. Before buying your pet Reeves Turtle, you need to prepare its caging, habitat, and even the basic needs of your pet. Prepare these

Chapter Three: A Suitable Habitat for Your Reeves Turtle

things before you even think of breeding, handling, or even taking your pet at home.

A conducive and cozy home will make a big part of your pet's life. It would also help your pet not become too stressed out in their life.

There are specific supplies that you need to buy and consider before you bring your Reeves at home. If you fail to provide these things, you would have a hard time balancing pet care and even buying these supplies.

The needed supplies are easily bought from certain pet stores and some, even in supermarkets. You need to make a trip to the supermarket before you go home and cross some things off the list.

In this part, we will help you set up the best house possible for your Reeves Turtle. Make a quick list of these things and go out and purchase these things!

Chapter Three: A Suitable Habitat for Your Reeves Turtle

Housing Needs

A habitat is a place where your Reeves Turtle lives. For turtles, their habitat is most terrarium or even aquarium. In this portion, you will learn how to set up a tank for your Reeves Turtle.

You need to set-up a great habitat for your pet because your turtle could easily outgrow its tank. You could set up a quick, simple, yet large habitat.

An aquatic turtle, such as your Reeves Turtle, would need clean water, proper lighting, proper heating, and even the right food. You need to focus on these things first before you even think of the plants, substrates, and other small fancy things. After you have these things set-up, you can now start on the decorations for your Reeves Turtle aquarium.

If you want to have more than one turtle, it is best to have separate enclosures or even specific portions for each pet.

Chapter Three: A Suitable Habitat for Your Reeves Turtle

What You Need to Set Up a Turtle Habitat

These are the definitely must-haves for your Reeves Turtle's enclosure:

- ✓ A big tank with a stand. You need to purchase a tank that is specifically designed to have water. You could use a fish tank, but not a tank that is suited for terrestrial reptiles such as desert tortoises and even iguanas. The aforementioned tanks can't really hold enough water inside.

- ✓ A basking area. The basking area must be a dry place where your turtle could sun-bathe itself. The basking process is important for your aquatic turtles to be healthy and survive the outside environment.

- ✓ Proper lighting. These lights should be enough to generate warmth. There are a lot of lights needed by your turtle inside the terrarium.

- ✓ Space Heaters. You need to one or more heaters to have the water in the turtle's aquarium at the correct

Chapter Three: A Suitable Habitat for Your Reeves Turtle

temperature. You should purchase heaters that is in plastic cages or heaters that are made from stainless steel. Your turtle could easily shatter glass heaters as well as get electrocuted and die.

- ✓ Thermometers. You should have two thermometers ready. The first one is used to measure water temperature and the other one is used to measure the air temperature at the basking area.

- ✓ System Filter. This filter will maintain the cleanliness of the water inside your turtle's aquarium. If you do not like to buy a filter, you need to frequently change the water inside the tank.

- ✓ Test strips or aquarium water test kit. This kit is used to check water quality as well as the water chemistry. You can start purchasing test strips, when you get a hang of it, you should buy the test kit because the latter are more accurate than the former.

Chapter Three: A Suitable Habitat for Your Reeves Turtle

There are also some other things that you can have, but you can go on without. These are:

- ✓ Substrate. The substrate is the things you put at the bottom of your turtle tank. Common substrates are Fluorite or gravel. If you plan to use live plants, you need to put a substrate. However, if you do not want to have plants in your tank, you do not really need a substrate.

- ✓ Aquarium Air Pump. This kind of pump would aerate the water. This pump would lessen the growth of anaerobic bacteria. Aside from this, your turtle likes the bubbles. If you have other animals with gills in the tank (such as fish or ghost shrimp), you need to have aeration or else your pets would die.

- ✓ Live plants

- ✓ Decorations such as aquarium background or artificial plants.

Chapter Three: A Suitable Habitat for Your Reeves Turtle

You need to prepare yourself, your house, and your house members if you plan to have a turtle. You need to create and take your time in creating a habitat that is conducive for your pet.

Building your pet's aquarium will be a great hobby. You would be the one to design the entire world of your Reeves Turtle! Make sure you thoroughly go through everything before you bring your Reeves Turtle at home.

Terrarium Starter Kits

If you want to raise your Reeves Turtle from the very start, you may need to purchase an aquatic turtle starter kit. These kits are easily available at your local pet stores. However, there are two major things that you need to think of when choosing a kit.

You need to know that your turtle will soon outgrow a small starter sized tank quickly. You need to have at least a 15-gallon tank to fully raise a hatchling, and at last a 20-gallon tank to raise at least two hatchlings.

Chapter Three: A Suitable Habitat for Your Reeves Turtle

However, if your turtle reaches the size more than 1.5 inch or 3.8 cm in terms of its carapace length, you need to create a bigger habitat for it. A key tip, a 15-gallon tank won't hold 15 gallons of water, unless you are willing to mount the basking area above it. If the basking area is inside the tank, you would lose around 1/3 to 1/2 water capacities.

If there is too little water in the tank, the water would easily be spoiled by your pet's pee and poo. It would be very unhealthy for your turtle, not only that, it would be very difficult to keep it clean.

Another thing that you need to look out for is the included items in the kit, as well as some other needed needs to complete your tank set-up. Some additional things include UVA and UVB light source, heater, and other important stuff.

Hatchling turtles need water temperature around 80 to 85 F or 26.7 to 29.5 C, until they reach the length of 1.25 inch or 3.2 cm.

If you are not planning to use a small-sized tank as a starter tank for your hatchling as its beginning habitat, you

Chapter Three: A Suitable Habitat for Your Reeves Turtle

need to make sure that you only put few amount of water when your pet is only a hatchling.

At this stage, the hatchling's lungs are not really well-developed yet, they need to have shallow water when they are still young. The shallow water would prevent them to drown if they get upside-down. If they drown, they might drown. It is okay if you want to start the habitat with a big tank, just start with a low water level and slowly raise it up when your pet lengthens.

Once your turtle develops its lung capacity, you can gradually increase the water - this would happen quickly. When you can see that your turtle could swim from the deepest point of the water up to the shore, you can start raising the water level gradually.

Your Reeves Turtle Habitat Inside the Tank

This part deals with the basics on how to set-up an indoor habitat that is found in a fish tank or an aquarium.

Most turtle owners would build outside pens such as ponds for their turtles. This is an excellent option if you have space, money, and the correct climate. However, some turtle

Chapter Three: A Suitable Habitat for Your Reeves Turtle

owners do not really like to build ponds, especially if they do not own the property.

Many aquatic turtle owners like to keep their reeves turtle indoors and then use tanks specifically designed for fish. Some owners use large storage containers, while some may use small-sized wading pools for kids, some may even have their tanks custom-made to fit specific designs for their homes. Some owners may even have indoor ponds for their pet reeves turtle, they would only do this if they have both money and space.

There are a lot of things that you need to do when you build your pet a habitat. The upcoming parts would look at some important factors.

Tank Size, Shape, and Type

When you are buying your tank, the first thing that you need to keep in mind is the ability of the tank to hold water inside.

This may be an obvious and silly idea. However, some tanks are only designed for terrestrial reptiles and they might break if you fill them with too much water. If the tank

Chapter Three: A Suitable Habitat for Your Reeves Turtle

breaks, it would make a huge mess. Make sure to purchase the tank that will hold water, such as a fish tank. If you want to use an old tank, make sure it will not leak.

Another important thing that you need to know is the size of the tank. If you have a good budget, you can get a tank that would be big enough for your turtle. It should be ten gallons of water equivalent to an inch of the turtle's carapace, especially when it reaches the full size. This method will ensure that you will not buy a bigger tank in the near future.

If your purchased tank is too small for your pet Reeves Turtle, it would be very difficult to clean. The water would be dirty much faster, this, then, would become smelly and unhealthy. Aside from that, your pet will not have enough room to swim in a small tank, and if you have more than one pet, they might fight.

You should also consider the shape of the tank that you will select. A 20-gallon tank may be a good idea for your turtle when it is very young, however, it will not give enough vertical swimming room for your turtle if it likes deep water.

Chapter Three: A Suitable Habitat for Your Reeves Turtle

Fortunately, your Reeves turtle is a poor swimmer. It needs a shallower tank which is safer and much better.

You also need to consider the deepness of water inside the tank. Make sure that the turtle could flip itself upright when it flips upside down in the water. The ratio should be 1:1. If the turtle is already 5 inches wide, it should have a 5 inches water depth inside the tank. If your pet Reeves Turtle could not flip itself over, it might probably drown and die.

Land Area / Basking Area

A basking area is a dry platform wherein your Reeves Turtle could sun themselves. Or if they are staying indoors, you need to have a basking lamp handy.

This basking area could be a commercially made turtle dock; it could be a rock or even just a log. Whatever you choose it will be, it should be comfortable for your pet to fit on, very easy for your Reeves Turtle to climb on to, and high enough for your pet not to get wet.

Chapter Three: A Suitable Habitat for Your Reeves Turtle

You can use a shelf-type, floating basking place as one of the easiest basking area for your pet Reeves Turtle. This basking area looks like a rock but is made of plastic.

This kind of dock is fairly easy to use. It will automatically adjust to the water level that you will put and will not waste much swimming space for your pet Reeves Turtle. This would be a great help for your pet because it is a poor swimmer.

You could also use a log or rock. If you want to use these things that you will get from nature, you need to boil these things first to kill any harmful microorganism, germs, or algae. Aside from that, you should never use anything with sharp edges because your Reeves Turtle could hurt itself.

You can also put an above-tank basking area. It will let you fill your Reeves Turtle aquarium near the top, which would give your pet more space to swim. You can buy a ready - made or you can make one yourself. A Plexiglas, which is made of wood, has an egg - crate light diffuser.

Chapter Three: A Suitable Habitat for Your Reeves Turtle

Tank Covers

Most turtle owners like to use heat-proof metal as their tank covers to put on the top of their tanks. These screens are fairly inexpensive as well as very important because this protects your turtle from things such as glass from an exploded lamp bulb. The bulbs that you will use for your Reeves Turtle aquarium might get very hot and might explode if they accidentally splashed with water. These covers will keep your turtles from ever climbing out of the tank, which they might do because they are confused with the outside world.

These tank covers could be placed on the tank to prevent older turtles from climbing out of the aquarium. Some turtles could do this because of the distance between the basking area and rim of the tank is very well in reach of your Reeves Turtle.

A word of caution, do not use Plexiglas or glass as a tank cover for your aquarium. These kinds of glass would filter out helpful UVB rays that your pet turtle needs in order to survive. Other than that, the heat from the lamps

Chapter Three: A Suitable Habitat for Your Reeves Turtle

inside the tank would cause the glass and plexiglas to either shatter or melt.

Some screen-type tank covers may block the light and heat to enter; you need to adjust the lighting. When the time comes that you need to remove the tank cover, such as feeding your turtle or cleaning the tank, make sure you replace the bulbs as soon as possible so it would not overheat the terrarium. If you will just leave it for a few minutes, turn off the lamps and move them farther away from the area to avoid the area being too hot.

You could also use a mesh screen that is very wide, or possibly, you can make yourself. Buy your mesh from a hardware store. The mesh screen would block less light.

Lighting

Lighting is another important thing that you need to know. Essentially, you are going to need lights that would give warmth, visible or artificial daylight, UVB, and UVA light.

Chapter Three: A Suitable Habitat for Your Reeves Turtle

Choosing a Tank Substrate

The thing that covers the bottom of the terrarium or the tank is called the substrate. There are a lot of choices on the best and even the worst substrates to choose from.

There is a not a real need for a substrate unless you are planning to use live plants. A bare bottom is the easiest to clean and would eliminate the possibilities that your pet would eat the substrate and would be injured by it. Remember, these things might happen to your pet.

Another easy option is using flat, large rocks. Remember, if you are going to take something from the wilderness, make sure to boil these things first to kill any germs or algae.

If you want to use live plants, except those plants that float, or you just want a substrate that would look nice or would create a natural environment, you have several choices:

- ✓ Fine Sand. This is a popular kind of substrate that many turtle owner likes. However, sand is very difficult to

Chapter Three: A Suitable Habitat for Your Reeves Turtle

upkeep even through frequent vacuuming. You could use sand if your turtle is natural digger. If you go with this option, make sure to use fine, clean sand, just like those sands that they sell for children sand boxes. Clean it thoroughly before you put it inside the tank. Make sure to frequently clean it once you have set up the habitat. If you do not clean them frequently, there might be debris and poops that would create a stinky, messy terrarium.

- ✓ Aquarium. This is another choice as a substrate for your turtle aquarium. This contains little to no nutritional value for your plants. In some scenarios, your turtle might even eat the gravel, unless the pieces are so smooth and the pieces are large enough for your pet not to eat them. However, it may not be work the risk.

- ✓ Fluorite. Fluorite might be the best choice if you plan to have plants for your turtle tank. This kind of substrate is a porous clay gravel, this is specifically designed to use in aquariums with plants. The fluorite could hold medium plants and it would make the terrarium attractive and natural. When you fill the tank with water, it may the water look like mud, just let it settle and let the filter run for a few days or with a polyester pillow stuffing. It may take a day or two to make the water clear again.

- ✓ Crushed coral. If you have a saltwater or brackish-water turtle, this kind of substrate is another good choice as a substrate. You can also use this as a partial substrate, which means you can mix it with another substrate, especially in a freshwater habitat. If you plan to use plants in your substrate, crushed coral is not a great choice of substrate.

Other Essential Things That You Will Need

Aside from the aforementioned things, there are still other things that you need to purchase for your turtle home. Some things include heater, or you may purchase two or more - in case one heater would stop working, thermometers

Chapter Three: A Suitable Habitat for Your Reeves Turtle

to measure the temperature inside the terrarium, habitat or tank stand, lights, and utilities to attach them. These things can be easily purchased at pet shops, especially those that sell reptile and aquarium supplies. Some of these things can be improvised or even be home-made.

Aside from physical shop, you can even find turtle supplies at different online stores.

Quality of Water

Your turtle is not really that sensitive to water quality unlike your fish. However, waste products will be stored in the tank and ammonia will be formed. This compound is pretty toxic and irritating to any pets even at low levels.

When you have successfully furnished your tank, some beneficial bacteria will grow in both the filters and tank. Some of these helpful bacteria will break down the ammonia which will be converted to other less harmful nitrates. After this process, water changes would also control the great change. However, before this whole cycle could

Chapter Three: A Suitable Habitat for Your Reeves Turtle

even take place, many by-products or bacteria would cause problems and even illness to your pet and its surrounding.

How to Measure Quality of Water

Measuring and monitoring the quality of the water inside the terrarium would help you catch early signs of condition inside the tank. You would know early on if there are harmful or irritating agents in the water. You can easily measure the quality of water using test kits easily available at pet stores.

You can easily use these kits at home and just follow the directions in the kit. The kit would also contain both the safe and the dangerous levels of ammonia, nitrites, and even nitrates. If ammonia, nitrite, or nitrate levels are too high, you need to have a complete water change of the tank. If the levels are creeping up or moderate, do a partial water change frequently.

Another thing that you need to consider is the pH balance inside the water, although this is not as grave issue as the waste product inside the tank.

Chapter Three: A Suitable Habitat for Your Reeves Turtle

Do I Need To Mind Chlorine in Water?

There are lot of different ideas on the usage of tap water and de - chlorinating it before putting it in the tank. Thankfully, turtles are not really sensitive to chlorine unlike amphibians or fish. However, it would still irritate them, especially the eyes.

If the water is still chlorinated, it will destroy the beneficial bacteria inside the tank. It would also affect the nitrogen cycle and the waste product breakdown. It is best to de - chlorinate the water before putting it inside the tank. You could use water conditioner that is easily available at pet stores.

Some pet owners would even use the chloramine to treat the tap water. If you can't find this, you should find a water conditioner that is used to remove chlorine. When using this conditioner, you need to allot at least 24 hours to fully take effect.

Chapter Three: A Suitable Habitat for Your Reeves Turtle

Salmonella Warning

You need to know the risks of salmonella and you need to take the necessary precautions especially when you are cleaning the filters and other turtle tank accessories, changing the waters, and even handling your pet Reeves Turtle.

The Correct Tank Size: How Big Should I Get?

Cleanliness and the water quality are easier to maintain if you own a larger tank. If there is only a small amount of water inside the tank, the waste products found inside is more concentrated.

If you have a larger tank, you need to do partial water changes. This task is more practical to maintain good water quality compared to changing a larger portion of water that is found in a smaller tank.

A general rule of thumb is 10 gallons of water per inch of your turtle.

Chapter Three: A Suitable Habitat for Your Reeves Turtle
The Filtration System

You have a lot of ways to filter your aquarium. For your turtles, you need to have a filter that is two to three times from the size of the turtle tank.

If you own a 20-gallon tank, you need to have a filter that is for 60 gallons, even if you do not plan to fully fill the tank. There are available filters with several different levels that are used to remove waste matters as well as by-products of turtles, these are also recommended. These kinds of filters could be biological, mechanical, and even chemical filtration.

There are pros and cons for different filter system; you need to know these things for you and your benefit.

Partial Water Changes

You need to regularly remove a part of the water and then replace it with fresh water; this act would dilute and remove the waste products found in the tank.

The frequency of these partial changes and the amount of water that you need to change will vary greatly on the factors, such as the size of tank, size of your pet turtles, and whether you feed your pet inside the tank.

Weekly or two to three times a week water changes would greatly help to keep the water quality high. You can use a siphon or a gravel vacuum to remove the wastes. These materials would help make the job easier; however, you should never siphon using your mouth, as this will increase your salmonella infection.

A Bare Bottom - A Good Choice

Having a bare bottom in your turtle tank would make it a lot easier to clean; the reason for this is that the uneaten food and wastes could not get trapped in rocks or any kinds of substrate.

You can use large gravel, i.e. those things that are too big to be eaten, and rocks for the bottom of your tank, this can make the tank attractive, but they are not really necessary.

Chapter Three: A Suitable Habitat for Your Reeves Turtle
A Separate Feeding Tank

Another way to reduce the amount of waste inside the tank is managing the tank itself. A good way to manage your turtle tank is through feeding your turtle in another container - but this is still a matter of your choice. You can use a storage container or a plastic tub as your feeding tank.

You can use the water from the main tank to ensure that the temperature of the water is just warm enough. Just remember to replace any water that you will get from the tank, this act would also be a partial water change for your pet.

A separate feeding tank would eliminate your problem of food decay inside the tank. Another thing, your turtle would like to eliminate wastes after eating, so if you have another tank, the amount of waste in the tank would also be reduced. You can just clean and sanitize the container after each feeding session.

A word of caution, hawing a separate tank for feeding would mean additional work and stressful episodes for your pet. A separate feeding tank is only recommended if you have a messy pet or give higher protein meals, or if you give food such as vegetables and greens inside the tank. If you have a great filtration system, you may feed your pet inside the tank. Pair your filtration system with routine water change and monitoring system.

Make sure you clean out excess food particles and do water changes before and after feeding your pet if you decide not to buy a feeding tank or container.

Cleaning your Turtle Aquarium

In this part, we will help you clean your aquarium. Cleaning the aquarium is an important task as this will eliminate both the wastes and chance of your pet being sick. These are the important things you need to have before you clean the tank:

- ✓ Clean cloths
- ✓ Bucket with 5 gallons of water
- ✓ Water conditioner
- ✓ Scrubber
- ✓ Thermometer
- ✓ Testing kits for aquariums

Chapter Three: A Suitable Habitat for Your Reeves Turtle

Tank Cleaning 101

When you are cleaning your tank, make sure that you attain the proper water temperature as well as the proper chemistry. Water quality should be your number one priority, as this will affect both the swimming and drinking of your turtle. Here are some steps on how to clean your turtle tank.

The Basics of Tank Cleaning

Before you even think of transferring your pet turtle in bucket or any temporary container, make sure that the container you have chosen has enough space for your turtle to roam and swim around. Always pick a size or two sizes larger than your pet, then put your pet.

Remove all the decorations inside the tank, such as the substrate, plants, rocks, and other ornaments, because you will need to clean it too. Put the decorations in a container and make sure it will not touch anything dirty or the floor.

Chapter Three: A Suitable Habitat for Your Reeves Turtle

Remember where you have originally put all the devices and ornaments inside the tank. Put them back to their original positions after you have cleaned the tank. This task would avoid the confusion for your pet turtle.

Need Help?

Here are some quick help tips that you might want to consider when you are cleaning the tank.

- ✓ The size of the tank should be bigger than your turtle. Your pet should be able to play and swim freely inside the tank. You need to follow the "rule of shell" for this task. Every inch of your turtle's hard outer shell should be around 10 gallons of water. For example, your pet has three inches of carapace; the chosen container should have a water capacity of 30-gallons.

- ✓ If you have more than one turtle, the tank size should be the size of the biggest turtle then add half of the volume of water that is in line of the length of the additional turtle's hard outer shell.

Chapter Three: A Suitable Habitat for Your Reeves Turtle
Put Your Turtle in another Clean Bucket

Put water in the clean bucket, make sure that the water is more than enough - this will enable your turtle to swim and also keep it hydrated. After this task, you need to move you turtle into this specific bucket.

When you transfer your turtle into this bucket, make sure you do it carefully and slowly, because your turtle might get hurt. In some cases, your turtle might bite you and it might hurt your hands. Handle your turtle gently but with great caution.

Make sure you have rocks and peats in the bucket so your turtle could have something to climb on.

Removing and Unplugging all the Heaters and Filters

Make sure that you have already unplugged all the heaters and filters before you take them away. You can put these in the sink, and make sure it is still clean. You can still clean these things without using detergent.

Chapter Three: A Suitable Habitat for Your Reeves Turtle

Cleaning the Tank

You need to put the tank outside of your house or in a sink or in a place where you are very comfortable. If you can't do the task alone, make sure you have someone else to help you.

See to it that the drain will not be clogged up by any solid object, such as debris or any shredded shells from inside the tank.

Slowly pour all the contents of the tank so you will not damage your tank. Use a scrubber and a piece of cloth to wipe and scrub all the debris that might get stuck on the tank's floors and walls.

Do not use a detergent, because it will make your pet sick due to the toxins inside of it. Detergents are known to damage your turtle's respiratory system.

When you are sure that the inside and outside of the tank are free of any debris, rinse the tank thoroughly (around three to five times). When you are sure that the tank is totally clean, pat dry with a piece of clean cloth, then put it back where it came from.

Chapter Three: A Suitable Habitat for Your Reeves Turtle

Cleaning the Ornaments, Substrates, and Devices

When you have finished cleaning your tank, it is now time to clean all the substrate, decorations, and any devices present in the tank. Remember; do not use any detergent when you wash these things. You just rinse these things thoroughly using running water to remove any dirt, soiled food, or any other debris. If you see that the dirt is still stuck there, scrub them lightly.

Putting Water inside the Tank

Make sure that you put a small drop of water conditioner to de - chlorinate water. Chlorine, as we have tackled, is very toxic to your pet Reeves Turtle. Make sure that there is no trace of chemical which is always in the tap water. Put water that is equivalent to half of the tank.

Putting Back the Ornaments, Substrate, and Devices

After cleaning the tank and putting new water, you can put cleaned heaters and filters where they are previously placed inside the tank.

Chapter Three: A Suitable Habitat for Your Reeves Turtle

You can return the ornaments and place them back on the exact spot where you have put them before. This would surely minimize stress for your turtle and to avoid great confusion.

The heaters and filters should run for an hour then test the water inside thank using test kits. Ideally, the pH level should be around seven and eight. The chlorine, ammonia, and nitrite level should only be zero. You should also note that the nitrate level should be not above 40 ppm. The tank's temperature should be around 70 to 75F or 21 to 26.6 C.

You could also buy additives from the local pet store if you could not control the chemical level inside the tank. These additives would help lower or raise the level of the element inside the tank.

Returning the Turtle Back in the Tank

When the water is in the correct chemical composition, coupled with the right level of temperature, you can return your Reeves turtle into its favorable spot.

Chapter Three: A Suitable Habitat for Your Reeves Turtle

After cleaning the tank, make sure to give a treat such as worm or its favorite food.

Cleaning the turtle's tank might take a whole time, but with the aide of your friend - you can make it easier. Set aside a day to clean the tank as well as all the decoration inside of it. This time could also be the time to know whether your turtle is in top shape.

This chapter has dwelt with all things that would make up a healthy and conducive environment for your Reeves turtle. Have these things ready before your actual tank clean-up, so you would not freak out during the cleaning task.

Cleaning the tank would eliminate bacteria and other harmful substances that could affect your pet.

Chapter Three: A Suitable Habitat for Your Reeves Turtle

Chapter Four: Meal Plan to Your Reeves Turtle

Good nutrition is an essential part of giving your pet a happy and healthy life. You need to know what is best for your pet and what not to give to your pet. You need to find the best food possible for your pet, to satisfy its needs and wants. Not giving the correct nutrition and food to your Reeves Turtle would greatly affect its health which may lead to diseases and even death.

Chapter Four: Meal Plan to Your Reeves Turtle

In this chapter, we will give you some food suggestion for your pet Reeves Turtle. These things are easily available and some might be easy to keep, buy these in bulk so you will not buy and buy.

Food for My Reeves Turtle

Fortunately, your Reeves Turtle is an omnivorous animal. Both commercial turtle food that is easily available, it could also accept plant and animal matter easily.

You could give worms, fish, insects, green leafy vegetable, aquatic vegetables, duck weed, water hyacinth, and water lettuce.

There are things that you need to look out for in the food for your turtle:

- 30%-40% protein
- Low fat content
- Vitamin D
- Calcium (Ca) to phosphate (Ph) ratio at least 2:1
- Vitamin and mineral supplementation

Chapter Four: Meal Plan to Your Reeves Turtle

Some Food Suggestions

When your Reeves Turtle is still a hatchling it will eat rapidly the food that you will offer it. Make sure that you will not overfeed your pet; you are recommended to feed it only once a day or every other day if you see that your pet is rapidly growing.

During this stage of its life, your Reeves Turtle is very carnivorous and will more likely to consume worms and insects and thawed frozen fish, but it would also eat any greens that you will feed it. You could also give aquatic vegetables such as duckweed.

When they begin to age, your pet would more likely eat vegetable. Some owners may opt to buy commercially available turtle diet.

As we have stated before, your Reeves Turtle are omnivorous animals. You could feed your Turtle crickets, waxworms, mealworms or even comet goldfish every few times a week. However, make sure that you place these things on the land area of the substrate and not the water part.

Chapter Four: Meal Plan to Your Reeves Turtle

You could also give your turtle every 3 or 4 times a week. Give your pet one to two teaspoons of leafy, dark greens such as collards, kale, or even mustard green. After a few hours, remove the uneaten vegetable after four hours.

Your turtle also likes canned turtle food, freeze-dried fish food, and even turtle pellets. These things are easily available at a pet store.

Aside from good food, you should also give good nutrition. Calcium supplements are essential for body growth and complete good health. A way to add calcium is through the food. Powdered calcium could be easily sprinkled to any food of your turtle.

You should give calcium supplement that is coupled with vitamin D3, especially if your pet is kept indoors. If you keep your pet inside the house, you just need to give calcium without vitamin D3.

You could also give cuttlefish bone, as long as you supervise the meal. This bone could be gnawed by your pet easily.

Multivitamins in a commercially prepared turtle diet is not really essential for your pet metabolism. If you decide

Chapter Four: Meal Plan to Your Reeves Turtle

to freeze your fish, it would eliminate the vitamin E. This vitamin is needed in maintaining a healthy pet.

We have just finished discussing the food that you can give to your Reeves Turtle. However, these are only starter meals that would make your pet happy and health as well. There are other variants available in the market if you want to try different things. However, you might need to contact your vet, other breeders, and your friends, to know more.

Do not worry; you will gain more knowledge as you go along your journey of being a Reeves Turtle owner. You need to carefully plan every meal and make sure you have enough food for your pet, especially during the days that you could not get out. It is not really advisable to starve your pet or to skip meals because you just forgot them. Remember, correct nutrition is an essential factor in determining good health for your pet.

Chapter Four: Meal Plan to Your Reeves Turtle

Chapter Five: Life Cycle of Your Reeves Turtle

Your pet turtle's life is quite complicated and as pet owners, you should know everything about your pet. You should know how it is raised up before you even think of breeding it.

Your turtle is an aquatic animal. Your turtle has a carapace or its outer shell, retractable head, a tail and four legs, which they can pull to the inside and outside of the shell whenever there is a predator. In some cases, they can even shut their shells to prevent predators from coming inside.

Chapter Five: Life Cycle of Your Reeves Turtle

Life Cycle

The First Step of Their Lives: Eggs

Some turtles usually lay their eggs on bed of moss or even in underwater. Most females like to dig holes in the mud or sand and then deposit their eggs in clutches. These clutches could be made up of one up to 100 eggs. After laying the eggs, the female will then bury the egg. Most mother turtles do not really stay near their eggs. The shell is easily pliable but leather and it will require the hatchling to used a specialized tooth - an egg tooth - to break away when it is ready to emerge, usually after 2 to three months.

The Second Step: Becoming a Hatchling

In some species, the gender of the hatchling is usually determined through temperature. In places where there is warmer temperature, the females could easy emerge from hatching eggs, while in cooler temperatures males would emerge.

As we have stated before, your hatchling will use an "egg tooth", it is a small white protrusion that is found on

Chapter Five: Life Cycle of Your Reeves Turtle

the nose, to be able to break through the shell and then directly go to the water.

Your Reeves Turtle could live in the water for a few years, they would eat animal and plant matter. Your turtle could also dig holes in dirt using their rough, strong feet to keep their cool. At this stage, your turtle would stay inside their shells to protect their bodies from ever drying out and also keep away the predators.

The Highlight: Turtle as Adults

When your turtle would reach the adult stage, it could live in either the water or land area. Your pet could also stay underwater for a period of time to swim but still need to emerge for water to get some air because your turtle have lungs unlike fishes which have gills.

Breeding Time

When your turtle senses that it can already breed, the male would rub up against the female or could also nod its head up and down, this is the way the males court the

Chapter Five: Life Cycle of Your Reeves Turtle

females. In some cases, the turtle may even bit the leg of the female or even bump the shells with her.

Females may carry out their fertilized eggs with them for more than a year; it could lay eggs one at a time. The parents would not be really involved in rearing the hatchling. During the courtship stage, your male turtle would swim and pursue around the turtle. It would tirelessly try to rub the snout of the female.

When the female is ready to lay its egg, the female turtle will go near low plants. You will not really see this act because they would dig their nests as well as shake some plants. When they lay eggs, the clutch would be around four to six eggs, and each egg would hatch about 90 days.

When the turtle has finally hatched, you should incubate the eggs at around 85 F. You will not regularly see the females laying their eggs, but you would see the hatchling pop from the egg shell.

Here is a simple guide on breeding your turtle:
- ✓ You need to winterize your turtle; most breeds do not really like to breed until it is fall.

Chapter Five: Life Cycle of Your Reeves Turtle

- ✓ Create a natural atmosphere that would mimic their nature, this would ensure that your turtle would really breed. You need to mimic the seasons that your turtle would normally feel when they are in the wild.

- ✓ You need to winterize your pet during the months of January up to February.

- ✓ Change the temperature in the terrarium between 50 and 60 degrees for around six weeks, after the number of weeks, return to the correct habitat temperature.

- ✓ Give a nice nesting area and the correct environment for your pet.

- ✓ Have a natural outdoor environment that would ensure you that you will have a successful and correct mating season. However, make sure that the environment could also work for you.

Chapter Five: Life Cycle of Your Reeves Turtle

- ✓ When you start creating an indoor environment for your turtle, make sure you have enough room to place 14 to 18 inches of soil in the bottom of the box, while still having enough room for your turtle. You could use sand or moss; just make sure to moist the environment from time to time. This would mimic the environment and ready your turtles to mate.

- ✓ After the successful mating of your turtle, your female would lay around two to 12 eggs.

- ✓ When she has laid the eggs, light mark the egg tops using non-toxic marker. Do not turn the egg from its original position; however, make sure that you put them in a separate container that would act as its incubator.

- ✓ Make sure that the mark is faced up, and not to turn over the egg.

- ✓ Incubate using the vermiculate.

Chapter Five: Life Cycle of Your Reeves Turtle

- ✓ Go out and buy a container of vermiculate at your local pet stores. Make sure to follow the instructions included in the box to mix it.

- ✓ When the vermiculate has been set, slowly place the eggs in the vermiculate.

- ✓ Seal the box with few air openings with the temperature inside of the box should be around 80 degrees, if possible.

- ✓ Wait for your eggs to hatch.

- ✓ The process of hatching should be around 80 to 150 days.

Some Facts about Your Hatchling/ Young Turtle:
- ✓ Your pet turtle would grow at a very slow rate, but the time spent would not really take toll on their bodies. In most cases, the organs of a young turtle are just the same as the organs of old turtles.

Chapter Five: Life Cycle of Your Reeves Turtle

- ✓ The turtles are considered to be one of the longest-lived species. The largest species could live the longest. Some turtles could only live for 11 years, but some could live more than 100 years.

These are just some things that you need to know about the life cycle of your Reeves Turtle. And, if ever you plan to breed them, make sure that you have enough time, money, and resources to do it. Remember, breeding your turtles would not mean money, it would just mean continuing the lineage of your pet.

Chapter Six: Keeping Your Reeves Turtle Healthy

Having a pet would not only deal with all the positive side, such as preparing the household, food, and even breeding. Having a pet would mean dealing with all the negative stuff that would come through.

You need to be ready when sickness comes to the life of your pet. Make sure you are ready financially as well as setting aside your time. You need to be strong for both you and your pet in order to overcome this obstacle.

Chapter Six: Keeping Your Reeves Turtle Healthy

Inspect the Turtle Aquarium

Most health concerns could be rooted from the incorrect turtle aquarium practices as well as poor water quality.

Your turtle literally lives in its own turtle. You need to provide everything and make sure that their toilet bowl is very clean and can be easily cleaned.

The pet turtle industry has been alive for a long time, and many turtles have fully adapted to new kinds of habitat. With many kinds of species worldwide, there is a general guideline that you could follow to prevent medical problems.

Here are some steps to help you keep your turtle in great shape for a long time.

Have a Healthy Home for your Reeves Turtle

- ✓ It is not acceptable now to have a habitat made of a little plastic bowl for your pet reeves turtle.

- ✓ Make sure that you greatly consider the tank size. The correct size of tank is determined through the number

Chapter Six: Keeping Your Reeves Turtle Healthy

and the size of your pet turtles. The larger size or even a bigger number of turtle would need a bigger size of tank.

- ✓ If the tank is too small, the balance would be off and there would be too much waste product in the water and would cause stress for your pet.

- ✓ If you have a stressed turtle, it would have a compromised immune system; soon enough, your pet would be more prone to infection.

- ✓ The main problem of having too large of a tank would just be finding the food inside the tank.

- ✓ You have other choices if you do not want to use fish aquariums as your turtle habitat. You can use any container that is able to hold water.

- ✓ You can have outdoor habitats, even only during warmer months.

Chapter Six: Keeping Your Reeves Turtle Healthy

- ✓ In whatever kind of tub or container that you would want to use, remember, cleaning is the key to keeping your turtle happy and satisfied in the terrarium.

Giving Warmth to your Turtle

- ✓ Your turtle are ectothermic animals, which mean they need an outside heat source to have the correct body temperature to have optimum physiological function.

- ✓ You need to have two kinds of heating systems inside your tank, the first one, namely, is having a basking lamp.

- ✓ Basking lamp is used to stimulate heating directly from the sun and it would encourage your pet to go out of water to thoroughly dry its shell.

- ✓ You also need to water. However, this is not really important because your Reeves Turtle does not really spend too much time in water.

Chapter Six: Keeping Your Reeves Turtle Healthy

- ✓ You need to set-up a correct temperature gradient within the terrarium, your turtle would be the one to choose in what spot it wants to spend its time.

UV Lights Are Essential for a Healthy Life

- ✓ UV lights, or Ultraviolet Lights, are very important for the correct calcium absorption of your pet.

- ✓ UV and calcium are very important to growing, young turtles, but this would benefit greatly your pet at any age.

- ✓ Do not skip the necessary lighting in the terrarium, without the correct lighting source, your turtle could have the correct bone and shell health.

- ✓ If you can't provide the correct lights, you might want to keep your turtle outside, because your turtle would benefit from the natural UV rays.

Chapter Six: Keeping Your Reeves Turtle Healthy

- ✓ If you do not have enough space for outdoor habitat, make sure you get the correct UVB lights.

Having the Correct Nutrition
- ✓ Giving the correct nutrition is a big part of your turtle's health.
- ✓ You should thoroughly learn the health requirement that is vital for your Reeves Turtle.
- ✓ Mineral and vitamin supplements are essential to the diet of your Reeves Turtle.
- ✓ Have fresh water for your turtle for drinking water.
- ✓ Make sure that you remove all uneaten food after a couple of hours. This is to maintain the water quality inside the terrarium.

High Water Quality inside the Terrarium
- ✓ Feces and any uneaten food could terrible contaminate the water quality.

- ✓ You need to have enough filtration and change water frequently.

Chapter Six: Keeping Your Reeves Turtle Healthy

- ✓ The filters within the terrarium should be suited for the size of the tank. Make sure that you ask your vet on the correct filter and amount of filters you need.

- ✓ You should regularly maintain the filters and even the terrarium and then keep the water clean.

- ✓ Your terrarium should not have a pungent smell. Make sure that there is no bad odor that is coming from the water.

- ✓ Always check the filter and make sure that it is clean.

- ✓ You can do slow partial water changes over a period of time.

- ✓ You could also treat the water with de - chlorinators or conditioners. Your turtle is not really sensitive with chlorine, so you could use a small bit.

Chapter Six: Keeping Your Reeves Turtle Healthy

Handling and Grooming

Keep these things in mind whenever you're handling your pet and keeping them hygienic:

- ✓ Always wash your hand before and handling your pet Reeve's turtle. This step is required for both you and your pet. You would not want to contract disease from your pet nor transmit disease to it.

- ✓ These other information should be taken with caution. Please consult your veterinarian first before doing any other steps. Other pet owners like to trim the beak and nails of their pet Reeve's turtle.

- ✓ Keep in mind that your captive Reeve's turtle has changed environments. They do not have rough roads to keep their beaks and nails trimmed.

- ✓ The downside of not trimming its nails and beak is that it will develop an overbite. Trimming nails and

Chapter Six: Keeping Your Reeves Turtle Healthy

beak is a two person task, ask assistance from your vet, or if you are experienced enough, ask assistance from your friends.

- ✓ Turtle nails tend to overgrow because they do not wear them off too often, especially if you just keep them inside their tank. Clipping your turtle's nail is important as it may get stuck in a carpet of filer, or even might tear the claw with the toe still stuck to it. Trimming turtle's nails are just the same as other pets. Just do not feed them days before the procedure and make sure you handle them with extreme care.

- ✓ Trimming beaks is a new task for novice pet turtle owners. Since they do not have rough things or dirt to chew on, their beaks will just grow and maintain its length.

- ✓ You can give your pet Reeve's turtle cuttle fish bone as a chew toy; this will serve as a pre-trimming

Chapter Six: Keeping Your Reeves Turtle Healthy

procedure. On the procedure day, make sure to use a paper fingernail file will not hurt your Reeve's turtle.

Here are some steps that you need to take when trimming the beak and nail:

- Do not feed your turtle for a couple of days.

- Take good care when handling your pet turtle. Make sure you have a towel and the necessary materials with you.

- If you are alone, sit down, hold the turtle between your thighs and place them over the towel.

- Make sure you get the turtle to poke its head out. You might need to convince your pet turtle to coax its head out.

- You might need to train your pet turtle to have its head touch.

Chapter Six: Keeping Your Reeves Turtle Healthy

- Hold the turtle's head/hand side by side; never put too much pressure to your pet turtle as you may injure it.

- Trim the nails and beak slowly but surely. It might take a while, but make sure your pet turtle is comfortable in this process.

Handling your pet Reeve's turtle is very different from other animals. Take great caution when you are handling them. Just like any other mammals or household pets such as cats, dogs and even snakes, turtles should be socialized at a young age. This could be a great way for them to learn to socialize with new people and be relaxed when they have companion with them.

Most Reeve's turtle are great for beginners because they are one of the most docile turtles out there. They can be easily trained and task to learn new tricks.

Handling them actually depends on how domesticated these animals are, so if you acquire a baby Reeve's Turtle or it was born captive they will be easier to

Chapter Six: Keeping Your Reeves Turtle Healthy

handle and tame since you as the keeper can introduce them the concept of socialization. Regularly touching them while they are still young will make them get used to you and your scent. You need to set a rule that you are their owner and learn to earn their trust so they could follow your command easily.

Here are some guidelines for you to follow when handling your pet turtle:

- Use two hands when you pick up your turtle. Use each hand on each side of the shell, preferable between the back and front legs. It is not a surprise that turtles are good in wiggling out of any situation, some even kick, claw, or even bite.

- Do not try to pick up the turtle using its tail. It can potentially dislocate some bones which is very painful for your pet turtle.

- Rotate your turtle head over tail (or tail overhead) rather than doing it side over side when you want to

Chapter Six: Keeping Your Reeves Turtle Healthy

inspect its bottom shell. If you turn your turtle from side to side, it could cause your intestine to twist, which could lead to your pet's death.

- Do not keep your turtle on its back when not necessary. This position is very stressful and unnatural for your pet. When turtles lie on their back, they are vulnerable to predators and feel out of control.

- Put your turtle down as gently as possible. This is to avoid injury to internal organs or its legs.

- Do not hold your turtle if it is still in young age especially on its shell. It can cause permanent damage to its body and shell.

- Do not strike or tap the shell against a hard surface. Also, do not injure the shell as it is a living tissue. This act will be very stressful for your pet.

Chapter Six: Keeping Your Reeves Turtle Healthy

- Do not move too much when you are holding your turtle. Remember that your pet is a living thing and may suffer from injury and stress when you move it too much. If you must, move smoothly and slowly.

Chapter Seven: Medical Problems of Reeves Turtles

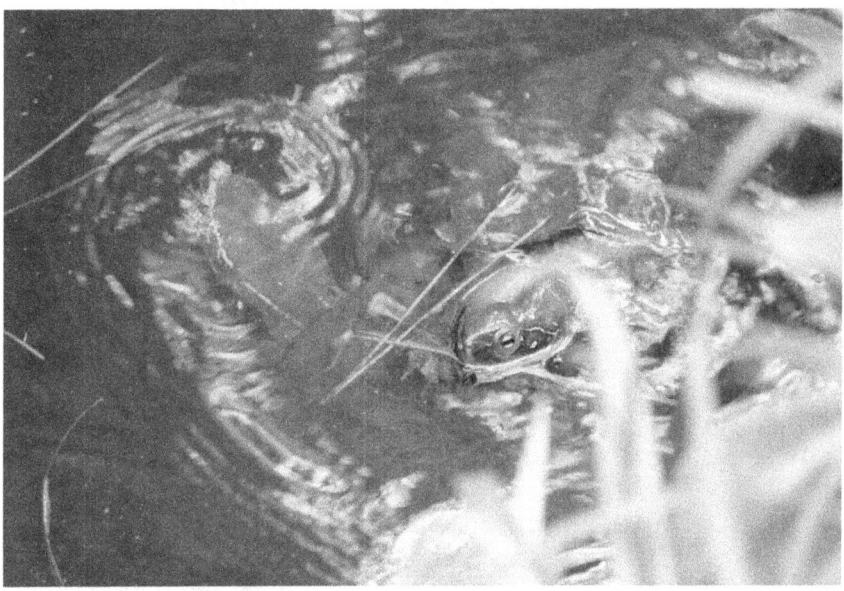

As a turtle owner, you should be a keen observation. Make sure that you catch all the problems early before these things could be very fatal.

Turtles are known to hide their symptoms until the disease has spread, most of the time; the early symptoms are very difficult to see. Make sure you know what is normal and what is not, in this way; you can see what is wrong with your pet easily.

Chapter Seven: Medical Problems of Reeves Turtles

If you see that there is something different about your pet, look around and see the husbandry. Is the tank clean enough? Are all the lamps still working? Is there enough food for a healthy nutrition? If you fix these things immediately, you might be able to avoid the other problems that your turtle might face.

Here are some common problems that your turtle might face in their lifetime:

Turtle Vitamin A Deficiency

Your turtle might not be getting enough vitamin A in their nutrition. The first sign for this is a swollen eyelid. If you do not do enough testing, the sign could be the same as eye infections.

Do not fret; this deficiency is easily fixed with a vitamin A treatment. Make sure that you give your pet a good diet to prevent this problem.

Chapter Seven: Medical Problems of Reeves Turtles

Aural or Ear Abscesses in Turtles

There looks like a purulent material that will build up under the tympanic membrane. There would also be a swelling on the side of the head. Both vitamin A deficiencies and unsanitary water condition are a big part of aural abscesses.

The main prevention for this problem is the right diet and clean diet. The treatment for this problem is only a minor surgery. However, there must be underlying condition for this problem. You must know the cause and also to prevent this from happening again.

Respiratory Tract Disease in Turtles

The initial symbol of this kind of disease could only be as mild as a simple nasal discharge, increased mucus in the mouth, or even open mouth breathing.

In severe cases, this disease could cause some fluid build - up in the lungs, then would affect buoyancy and would cause the turtle to swim on one side.

Chapter Seven: Medical Problems of Reeves Turtles

Many turtle owners would think this disease is only connected to the bacterial infections; however there are also the same causes for the same causes.

Fungal, viral, and parasitic infections could all appear the same as the bacterial infection for a sick turtle.

Foreign bodies up a nostril, aspiration pneumonia, and cancer could also be other causes of these diseases.

As for the treatment, you should know the exact cause to treat your pet. There should be enough testing that would include culture, radiograph, cytology, and lung washes. Contact your vet immediately to know all your options and to make sure that your pet would be healthy again. Once the root cause of the problem is fully identified, then you could give the correct treatment.

For the initial prevention, you should do and give the correct husbandry because this disease affects many things.

Turtle Trauma

Turtle Trauma could be as simple as dropping turtle as a floor, falling over the tanks, getting crushed by rocks, being chewed on by dogs. Some might even include being

Chapter Seven: Medical Problems of Reeves Turtles

chewed by other turtles, turtles that are sucked into the filters, irritated by the other members inside the tank, burns from their lamps, and worn feet.

The treatment for this trauma greatly depends on how deep the lesion is. You must know the root cause to know if it is only mild or severe cases.

Some severe trauma might require you to have surgery for your pet, limb amputation, shell repair, medication, and antibiotics.

To prevent this problem, you must create a safe environment. You need to be sure that the basking area and the furniture are sturdy enough that it can't be tumbled down by your pet. You should have surfaces that are hard enough to give good traction, but also see that the surface is not too rough that it would damage the shell or even the skin.

Aside from this, your turtle is known to be an escape artist, they can climb almost anything. Make sure that you see that all escape routes are blocked off. Your dog could treat your turtle as a chew toy, so make sure that your other pets are away from your pet. You may also need to have

Chapter Seven: Medical Problems of Reeves Turtles

pest control in order to keep other pets, such as raccoons away from your yard. Know that there are other fish guards that you could put in the filters; this is to prevent turtles from being sucked in the filter. It's also recommended to separate aggressive playmates from the cage to avoid incidental fights.

Turtle Impaction

Turtle impaction can start as only ingesting foreign objects, which is a common problem for turtles. Some turtles might even incidentally swallow gravel that might clog their GI systems. They might also eat and swallow any rubber, metal, or plastic objects that would fit in their mouths.

Small objects could easily pass in their bodies, but if the pieces inside your turtle are big, it might need medical intervention such as surgery. To prevent this problem, make sure that you thoroughly check the husbandry, if you see the problem, make sure that you alter it immediately.

Chapter Seven: Medical Problems of Reeves Turtles

Turtle Egg - Binding

The medical term for the difficulty of giving birth, which may be due to egg binding, is called as Dystocia. Your female turtles are able to produce eggs even if they are without a male companion. If there is no intrusion, your female turtle could lay her eggs without any problems. However, if your turtle is kept in a cage, it might have a slight problem.

Some turtles will lay their eggs easily in the water o even in basking sites. But, some might hold on to their eggs until there is a medical intervention, like surgery. For the prevention of this case, make sure you have enough egg-laying area in your turtle terrarium.

Turtle Shell Lesions

Some causes of the shell lesions include inadequate heat, poor water quality, inadequate basking spots, stress, burns, and even rough substrate.

The symptoms for this will vary from mild irritation and superficial redness up to foul odor, soft spots of rotten bone, while some might even lead to death.

Chapter Seven: Medical Problems of Reeves Turtles

The initial treatment for this scenario is an aggressive surgical debridement, antibiotics, and culture of the infected bone for a long period of time.

To prevent this problem, you should observe and see your husbandry. Give enough water of great quality, adequate heat and lighting, and strategic placing of these things inside the terrarium.

Other Problems That Your Pet Might Face

If you have given your pet appropriate diet and housing, your Reeves turtle would be energetic and active inside the turtle terrarium. However, just like any animals inside the tank, diseases and illnesses will affect them. Here are some indicators that your turtle is experiencing something:

- Sunken or swollen eyes
- Inability to submerge or listing
- Frothing or gaping at the mouth
- Bubbling in the nose area
- Refusal to enter water

Chapter Seven: Medical Problems of Reeves Turtles

- Excessive basking
- Refusal or inability to
- Irregular or assymetrical growth
- Open wounds on the shell or skin
- Obvious discoloration
- Any other abnormal appearance or behavior

If you see a symptom that is listed above, you should immediately seek vet assistance because it is necessary. Find a vet that specializes in tortoises and turtles, or at least exotic animals or reptiles. Some common diseases of your Reeves Turtle might include:

- Respiratory diseases
- Abscesses
- Vitamin A deficiencies
- Fractures
- Parasites
- Shell infections

Chapter Seven: Medical Problems of Reeves Turtles

Some signs of these diseases might include…

Roundworms commonly known as internal parasites are very common for Reeves Turtle. In most cases, these infections have really no clinical sign. These are usually detected through routine fecal exam.

In severe cases, your turtle might experience severe weight loss and even diarrhea.

Some tell-tale signs to know that your turtle is sick are…

Certain signs of specific diseases for your Reeves turtle greatly vary. Some symptoms might include nasal discharge, especially in respiratory infection.

What is the best first aid for turtle diseases?

There are different solutions for different problems. Your pet needs to undergo several tests to fully know the disease of your pet, especially because your pet does not really talk and it can't tell the vet the specific problem.

Vitamin A Deficiency is usually solved with either injected Vitamin A supplement or some could be taken

Chapter Seven: Medical Problems of Reeves Turtles

orally. However, the treatment should only be done under the supervision of your vet, especially for hypervitaminosis A. This is a condition that is a result of both over dosage and incorrect usage of the Vitamin A. When there is vitamin A deficiency, you should improve or correct the diet of your Reeves Turtle.

For infections in the respiratory system, we must know that these things are often caused by bacteria. Most of these turtles also have Vitamin A deficiency which should also be treated.

Your vet would recommend x-rays (also called radiographs) blood cultures and tests. These things are needed to know the root cause of the infection. The basic treatment for this kind of infection usually revolves around giving antibiotics. These antibiotics could be given as injections, orally, or possibly as nose drops. Once your turtle gets sick, it will need intensive care which will include force feeding in the vet clinic and even fluid therapy.

For the case of abscesses, these things should only be treated surgically. Once the abscess is opened up, the pus inside the abscess is drain and the affected tissues will be

Chapter Seven: Medical Problems of Reeves Turtles

cleaned with a medicated cleansing solution. In some cases, there might need to culture the abscess to fully know what type of bacteria cause this specific type of abscess. Injected or oral antibiotics, topical medication may also be required for the abscess problem.

Remember, you need to seek immediate vet care if you see that there is a slight change from the normal, especially if you see that your pet is lethargic.

Shell fractures could be easily fixed by your trusty vet. However, the infections for this kind of fractures are very challenging to treat. To treat this problem, you need to know the kind of organism, such as bacteria, virus, or fungus is causing this grave problem. You should thoroughly clean the shell using the appropriate antibiotic that is also suited for your pet.

Parasites are easily treatable with simple deworming medication. You first need to identify the parasite that is affecting your pet. The identification can be done through microscopic fecal exam; this will determine what kind of drug will be needed in the procedure.

Chapter Seven: Medical Problems of Reeves Turtles

Prevention is the Key to All

As we have discussed before, poor husbandry is one or the trigger of the medical problems for your pet. Remember, prevention is better than cure.

Make sure you have a thorough research before you want to buy a pet. Aside from that, make sure you give all the necessary things that your turtle might need.

Turtles with enough love and care could live a long time. Remember, your turtle live in their own site as toilet. However, you should just follow the correct husbandry guidelines, observing signs of problems, having great water quality, and going to your vet when problems start to occur.

This chapter has dealt with the problems that your pet Reeves turtle might face in the future. As we have said before, one of the primary reasons for your pet to get sick is due to husbandry problems. Know that you should always look and see if the husbandry is still okay. If there is an off balance inside the husbandry, immediately fix it to prevent any problems.

Chapter Seven: Medical Problems of Reeves Turtles

Aside from that, you should also know what is normal for your pet. You should know all the bumps and spots of your pet turtle, if there is something wrong, immediately fix the problem to prevent any illnesses in the future.

If you see that there is something wrong with your pet, remember to seek vet attention immediately. Do not try to home medicate because you might just worsen your pet's condition.

Conclusion

The whole book has thoroughly discussed the ins and outs of your Reeves Turtle. We surely believe that these things are enough to arm you to become the best Reeves Turtle owner in your area.

A great thing about having turtles is they are very to take care of. You just need to set up the correct housing and you are good to go. However, this housing would need your blood and soul. You should design a tank that is specifically

Conclusion

for your pet. The chosen tank must mimic the natural environment so your pet could always be at ease.

Keep in Mind!

Turtles are known to live a long life, make sure that you are ready to commit to take care of this pet. Remember, they could live up to 50 years! A key to keeping a happy and healthy turtle is providing it with good feeding, housing, and taking care of it especially during its illnesses.

A sustainable house is also important to your pet. Make sure that your pet is comfy and happy inside the terrarium. Know that the substrate of your choosing is a great part of the terrarium, choosing a harsh one might destroy the shell or skin of your pet, however, if you have soft substrates, your pet might get enticed to eat it and it might get impacted in the GI system.

Having a complete home is not an easy task; you must purchase high quality things that you know would surely help your pet. Also, you need to know the correct

Conclusion

feeding for your pet. Incorrect diet would lead to diseases or even death.

You would not want to get in trouble while you are taking care of a pet. Illnesses for this pet could possibly be not only expensive but also heart - breaking.

Make sure that you know the insides and outs of your pet, although we have given you a lot, you should still look for more information about your pet. Remember, more information about your pet, the better. You need to master the ins and outs of your pet so you would give the best for your pet.

If you think you are up to this challenge, go out now and buy your very first Reeves turtle!

Conclusion

Glossary of Amphibian Terms

Acclimation – Adjusting to a new environment or new conditions over a period of time

Acrylic Aquarium – Glass aquarium alternative, usually lighter than an ordinary aquarium but can be easily scratched.

Active range – The area of activity which can include hunting, seeking refuge, and finding a mate

Ambient temperature – The overall temperature of the environment

Amelanistic – Amel for short; without melanin, or without any black or brown coloration.

Ammonia – made up of nitrogen and hydrogen. It has an unpleasant smell that's also toxic and corrosive. Leftover food in the enclosure can be contributing factors that build up ammonia

Anerythristic – Anery for short; without any red coloration.

Aquatic – Lives in water.

Arboreal – Lives in trees.

Bacteria – microorganisms that are distributed widely in the environments. Turtle keepers should be aware of the harmful effects of bacteria

Bacteria Bloom – sometimes referred to as a tank syndrome.

Basking – a procedure where tortoises or turtles warms or dries up their body. Tortoises/turtles will need to have a basking area at a certain temperature to prevent shell rot. It also allows absorption of UVA and UVB for thermoregulation

Betadine – An antiseptic that can be used to clean wounds in reptiles

Bilateral – Where stripes, spots or markings are present on both sides of an animal.

Biotic – The living components of an environment.

Bridge – part of the shell that's located in the middle of the front and black legs connecting the top and bottom shell.

Brumation – The equivalent of mammalian hibernation among reptiles

Cannibalistic – Where an animal feeds on others of its own kind.

Cloaca – also vent; a half-moon shaped opening for digestive waste disposal and sexual organs.

Cloacal Gaping – Indication of sexual receptivity of the female.

Cloacal Gland – A gland at the base of the tail which emits foul smelling liquid as a defense mechanism; also called Anal Gland.

Clutch – A batch of eggs.

Constriction – The act of wrapping or coiling around a prey to subdue and kill it prior to eating.

Crepuscular – Active at twilight, usually from dusk to dawn.

Diurnal – Active by day

Drop – To lay eggs or to bear live young

Ectothermic – Cold-blooded. An animal that cannot regulate its own body temperature, but sources body heat from the surroundings

Endemic – Indigenous to a specific region or area.

Estivation – Also Aestivation; a period of dormancy that usually occurs during the hot or dry seasons in order to escape the heat or to remain hydrated.

Flexarium – A reptile enclosure that is mostly made from mesh screening, for species that require plenty of ventilation.

Fossorial – A burrowing species.

Gestation – The period of development of an embryo within a female.

Gravid – The equivalent of pregnant in reptiles

Gut-loading – Feeding insects within 24 hours to a prey before they are fed to your pet, so that they pass on the nutritional benefits

Hatchling – A newly hatched, or baby, reptile.

Herps/Herpetiles – A collective name for reptile and amphibian species.

Herpetoculturist – A person who keeps and breeds reptiles in captivity

Herpetologist – A person who studies ectothermic animals, sometimes also used for those who keeps reptiles.

Herpetology – The study of reptiles and amphibians.

Hide Box – A furnishing within a reptile cage that gives the animal a secure place to hide.

Husbandry – The daily care of a pet reptile.

Hygrometer – Used to measure humidity.

Impaction – A blockage in the digestive tract due to the swallowing of an object that cannot be digested or broken down.

Incubate – Maintaining eggs in conditions favorable for development and hatching.

Juvenile – Not yet adult; not of breedable age

LTC – Long Term Captive; or one that has been in captivity for more than six months.

MBD – Metabolic Bone Disease; occurs when reptiles lack sufficient calcium in their diet.

Morph – Color pattern

Musking – Secretion of a foul smelling liquid from its vent as a defense mechanism.

Oviparous – Egg-bearing.

Ovoviviparous – Eggs are retained inside the female's body until they hatch.

Popping – The process by which the sex is determined among hatchlings.

Probing – The process by which the sex is determined among adults.

Sloughing – Shedding.

Sub-adult – Juvenile

Substrate – The material lining the bottom of a reptile enclosure.

Stat – Short for Thermostat

Tag – Slang for a bite or being bitten

Terrarium – A reptile enclosure.

Thermo-regulation – The process by which cold-blooded animals regulate their body temperature by moving from hot to cold surroundings.

Vent – Cloaca

Vivarium – Glass-fronted enclosure

Viviparous – Gives birth to live young.

WC – Wild Caught

WF – Wild Farmed; refers to the collection of a pregnant female whose eggs or young were hatched or born in captivity.

Yearling – A year old.

Zoonosis – A disease that can be passed from animal to man.

Photo Credits

Page 10 Photo by user Denise Chan via Flickr.com, https://www.flickr.com/photos/denn/4481279876/

Page 13 Photo by user Sek Keung Lo via Flickr.com, https://www.flickr.com/photos/losk/14212478104/

Page 30 Photo by user Denise Chan via Flickr.com, https://www.flickr.com/photos/denn/2453395693/

Page 64 Photo by user Denise Chan via Flickr.com, https://www.flickr.com/photos/denn/4480632939/

Page 69 Photo by user Anguskirk via Flickr.com, https://www.flickr.com/photos/anguskirk/18001251948/

Page 78 Photo by user Mark Lehmkuhler via Flickr.com, https://www.flickr.com/photos/mark_lehmkuhler/30250031230/

Page 93 Photo by user Masaoki Mitsutake via Flickr.com, https://www.flickr.com/photos/masa-ok/7208730856/

Page 108 Photo by user Denise Chan via Flickr.com, https://www.flickr.com/photos/denn/18634863/

References

Chinese Pond Turtle – Encyclopedia of Life

http://eol.org/pages/4520624/details#distribution

Reeve's Turtle - Petguide.com

https://www.petguide.com/breeds/turtle/reeves-turtle/

Chinese pond turtle (Mauremys reevesii) - Arkive.org

https://www.arkive.org/chinese-pond-turtle/mauremys-reevesii/

Reeve's Turtle Care - Reptilesmagazine.com

http://www.reptilesmagazine.com/Reeves-Turtle-Care/

Tempted to Get a Pet Turtle or Tortoise? Read This First - Vetstreet.com

http://www.vetstreet.com/our-pet-experts/tempted-to-get-a-pet-turtle-or-tortoise-read-this-first

Reeve's Turtle – Perfect Pet Turtles for Red Eared Slider Fans – ThatPetPlace.com

http://blogs.thatpetplace.com/thatreptileblog/2013/08/05/reeves-turtles-ideal-pet-turtles-for-red-eared-slider-fans/

Reeve's Turtle Care Sheet - Reptilecentre.com

https://www.reptilecentre.com/info-reeves-turtle-care-sheet

How to Set Up an Aquatic Turtle Tank – MyTurtleCam.com

https://www.myturtlecam.com/habitat.php

What Do I Feed My New Turtle or Tortoise? – PetSmart.com

https://www.petsmart.com/learning-center/reptile-care/what-do-i-feed-my-new-turtle-or-tortoise/A0082.html#feeding_turtle

How to Clean a Turtle Tank in 8 Simple Steps - Aquaristguide.com

https://aquaristguide.com/how-to-clean-a-turtle-tank/

Keeping the Water in Your Turtle Tank Clean – TheSprucePets.com

https://www.thesprucepets.com/keeping-water-in-your-turtle-tank-clean-1238362

How to Breed Turtles – Cuteness.com

https://www.cuteness.com/article/breed-turtles

Turtles - Aquatic – Diseases – VCAHospitals.com

https://vcahospitals.com/know-your-pet/turtles-aquatic-diseases

9 Reasons Why You Should Have a Turtle as a Pet - TheOdysseyOnline.com

https://www.theodysseyonline.com/9-reasons-why-you-should-have-turtle-pet

Reeves Turtle (Chinese Pond Turtle) – AllTurtles.com

https://www.allturtles.com/reeves-turtle-5/

www.ingramcontent.com/pod-product-compliance
Lightning Source LLC
Chambersburg PA
CBHW060841050426
42453CB00008B/778